Looking Around

Acknowledgments

Executive Editor: Diane Sharpe
Supervising Editor: Stephanie Muller
Design Manager: Sharon Golden
Page Design: Simon Balley Design Associates
Photography: Greg Evans: page 11 (right); Chris Fairclough:
page 19; Robert Harding: page 11 (left); Last Resort Picture Library:
page 13; Stock Boston: (John Coletti) cover (middle right), (L. Migdale)
cover (bottom right), pages 8, 17; Tony Stone Worldwide: pages 7, 13;
Zefa: pages 21 (both), 27.

ISBN 0-8114-3721-3

Copyright © 1995 Steck-Vaughn Company.

1 2 3 4 5 6 7 8 9 00 PO 00 99 98 97 96 95 94

READ ALL ABOUT IT
STECK-VAUGHN

Looking Around

Paul Humphrey

Illustrated by

Maggie Downer

STECK-VAUGHN
COMPANY
ELEMENTARY · SECONDARY · ADULT · LIBRARY

We're walking
to the park to
have a picnic.

Let's watch for the people and
places that are on our way.

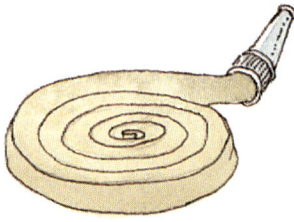

There's a fire engine!

Its siren is so loud!

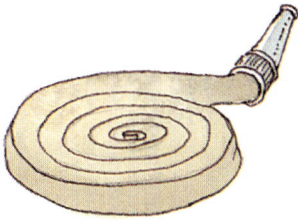

Firefighters must rush to put
out fires.

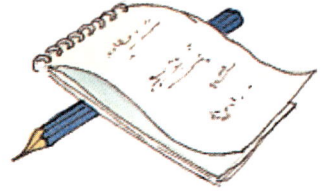

The police officer is helping
the girl.

Maybe she is lost.

9

Why is that bell ringing?

It's telling us that it's 12 o'clock.

10

Some buildings have big clocks on them so people can tell the time.

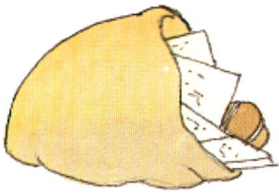

Look, the letter carrier
is taking the mail
out of the mailbox.

She empties the mailbox
every afternoon.

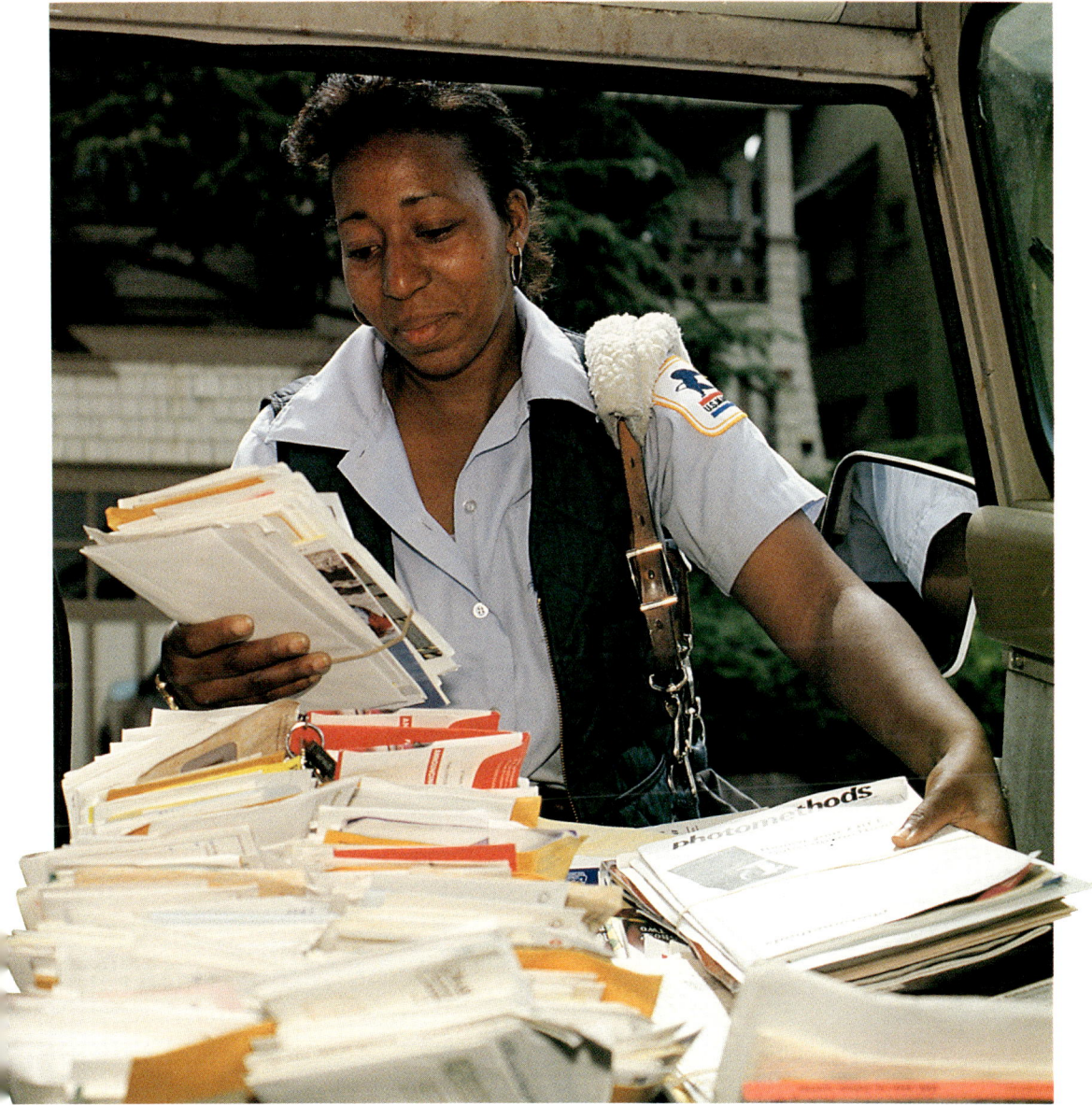

Then the mail is taken to be
sorted and delivered.

Here is the library.
I like to check out books.

14

My dad brings me to the library on Saturdays.

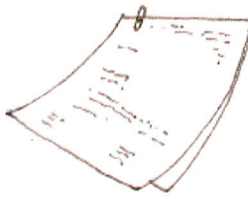

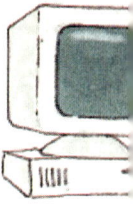

That building is the biggest one in town.

It's the town hall.

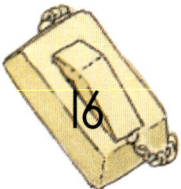

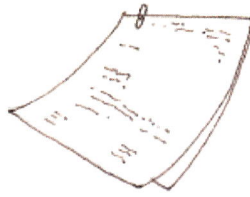

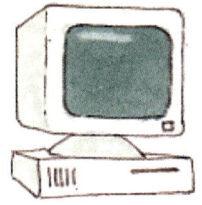

Every town has a town hall. Many people work there to make their town a great place to live.

The gardener is planting some flowers.

Let's have our picnic here by the pond.

We'll be able to see many different animals from here.

There are ducks and swans
swimming on the pond.

Let's play over by the statue.

22

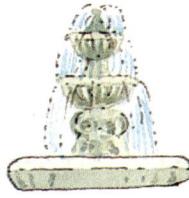

The writing tells us who she is.

Statues remind us of famous people.

We're going a different way back to your house.

There's our school.
It looks very quiet
on the weekend.

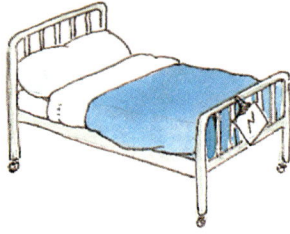

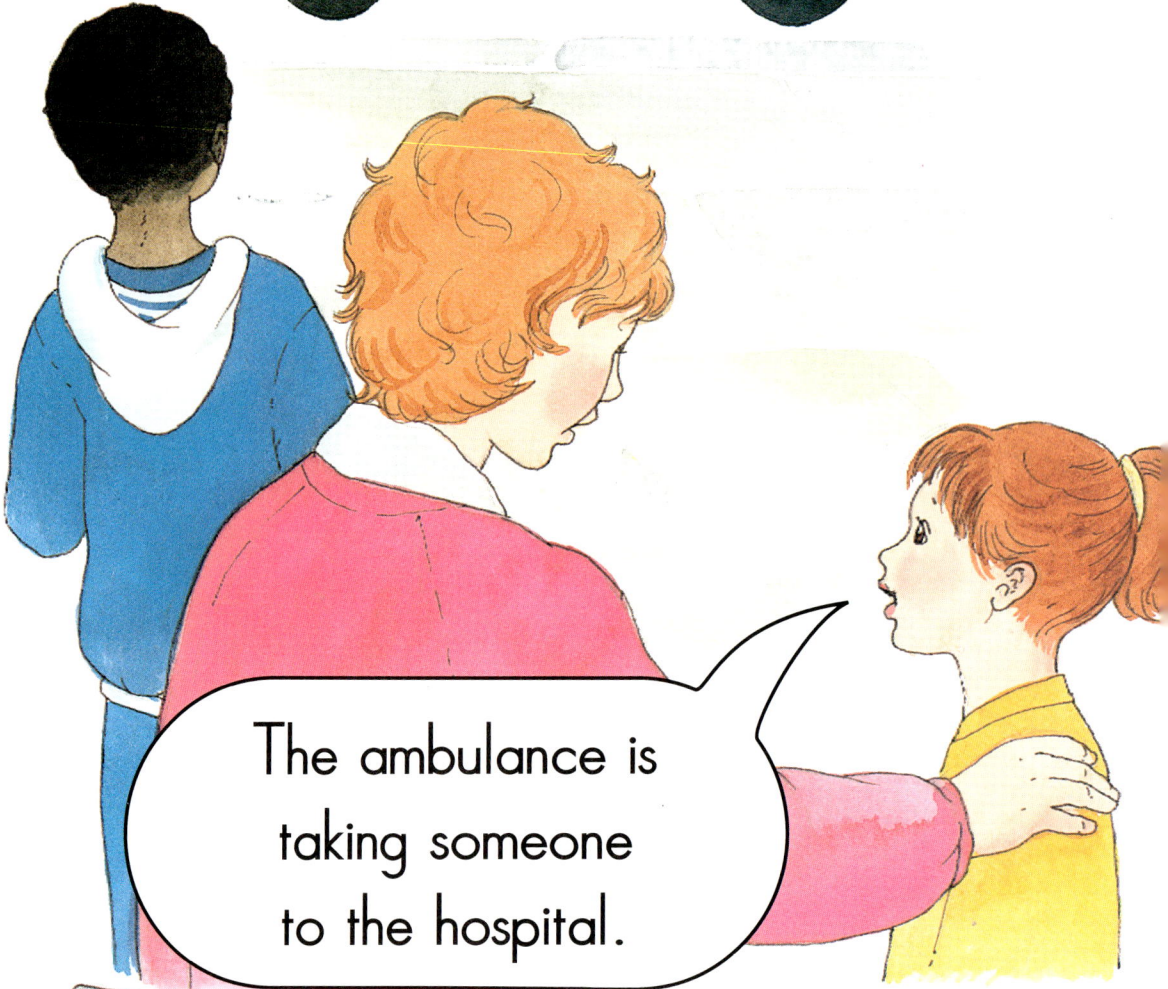

The ambulance is taking someone to the hospital.

Nurses work hard to help
sick people.

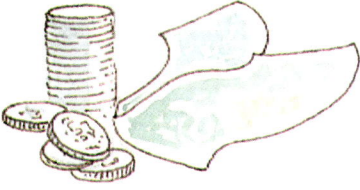

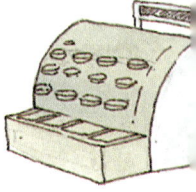

Let's do our shopping in this grocery store.

I'll let you choose something good for a snack!

29

Here is a picture of the town.
Can you name all the people
and places?

Index